THE TALYLLYN RAILWAY
60 YEARS OF PRESERVATION

TALYLLYN
preservation
60
1951 - 2011

THE TALYLLYN RAILWAY
60 YEARS OF PRESERVATION

David J. Mitchell

TALYLLYN preservation 60 1951 - 2011

© Talyllyn Railway Company 2011

All rights reserved. No part of this publication may be reproduced, stored in a retrieval system or transmitted, in any form or by any means, electronic, mechanical, photocopying, recording or otherwise, without prior permission in writing from Past & Present Publishing Ltd.

First published in 2011

British Library Cataloguing in Publication Data

A catalogue record for this book is available from the British Library.

ISBN 978 1 85794 367 2

Printed and bound in the Czech Republic
Silver Link Publishing Ltd
The Trundle
Ringstead Road
Great Addington
Kettering
Northamptonshire
NN14 4BW

ACKNOWLEDGEMENTS

Thanks are due to the many members of the TRPS who have provided the photographs and other assistance. Many of the pictures in the TR collection are anonymous and often undated, but the collection includes those taken by John Adams, John Slater and James Boyd. The archive provides a visual history of railway preservation, and is now being digitised and catalogued.

The two major books on the TRPS era, *The Chronicles of Pendre Sidings* and *Talyllyn Revived*, provide an invaluable record of what was done over the years, and the *Talyllyn News* and John Slater's newsletters record a great deal of detail.

Above all thanks are due to the thousands of volunteers and staff who have helped preserve, maintain and operate the TR over the last 60 years, without whose labours there would be no story to record. Photographs are credited where known, including those in the TR collection. Uncredited photographs are from the collections of the TR and the author.

The spelling of Welsh place names has changed over 60 years and current spellings have been used.

The text has been proof read by John Bate, Lawrie Bowles and Philip Sayers and their comments and corrections incorporated. The errors remain the author's responsibility.

TALYLLYN
preservation
60
1951 - 2011

Opposite: Tea break at Quarry with a North West Area gang in the autumn of 1955. Keith Walton and John Halliday, who would shortly form the Yorkshire Area, sit in the foreground, while on the right are Dorothy Boyd and the girls.

CONTENTS

Introduction	7
1 The 1950s: Early Days	9
14 May 1951: The First Public Train	13
1952: The Second Season	17
1953-1954	23
1955	40
1956-1960	44
2 The 1960s: Expansion and Consolidation	62
1964-65: Redeveloping Wharf	70
1965: The Centenary	73
3 1968-69: Rebuilding Abergynolwyn	79
Locomotive Developments	85
The 1970s: The Extension to Nant Gwernol	92
4 To The Present Day: Commemorations and Celebrations	107
21st-century Wharf	112
The TR Today	122
Index	128

THE TALYLLYN RAILWAY 60 Years of Preservation

What the TRPS is all about: a little train steaming along the Fathew valley, as it has for nearly 150 years. *Dolgoch* is heading a photographic charter train towards Brynglas against the snow-covered mountains of Snowdonia.

INTRODUCTION

The first train of the railway preservation era ran at 10.00am on Monday 14 May 1951 when Talyllyn Railway loco No 2 *Dolgoch* left Wharf station in Tywyn for the trip to Rhydyronen. This was the first train to be operated by a railway preservation society, anywhere in the world, and was the spark that was to lead to the worldwide movement of preserved railways. The story, however, starts earlier.

On 8 July 1950 the former MP for Merioneth, Sir H. Haydn Jones, died at the age of 85. An event that would normally have only attracted local attention led to national interest because Sir Haydn was one of those very rare people who owned a public railway. (Captain Howey of the Romney, Hythe & Dymchurch Railway was probably the only other such person at that time.) The Talyllyn Railway was one of only two narrow-gauge railways operating a timetabled service on the mainland of the United Kingdom. It was in a parlous state, with only one workable locomotive and still running its original 1866 rolling stock over the original track. It was a survivor of the Victorian era and was known and appreciated by enthusiasts.

Various people had given thought as to how the line might be 'preserved' in the event of Sir Haydn's death. L. T. C. (Tom) Rolt, the author and canal preservation pioneer, and Bill Trinder had already had a meeting with Sir Haydn. Others, including Owen Prosser, had written articles and letters. An article about the TR in the *Birmingham Post* a couple of years earlier had resulted in a letter to the paper by Tom Rolt, and a number of people had contacted him about the future of the TR.

Tom called a meeting at the Imperial Hotel in Birmingham on 11 October 1950, a few days after the last train had run on the TR. At that meeting the Talyllyn Railway Preservation Society was formed and a committee appointed, which would have discussions with Sir Haydn's widow; this resulted in Lady Haydn agreeing to hand over the railway to the TRPS with effect from 8 February 1951. The pattern set by the TRPS of the society providing labour and funds to maintain and restore the railway has been followed by most subsequent railway preservation schemes. At the time many enthusiasts would have liked to have preserved the Ffestiniog Railway, which was in a much better condition, but obtaining control of the FR would have been much more difficult.

The TRPS faced two major difficulties at the start: first, having a locomotive to work the train, and second, having serviceable track on which to run the train. The pictures that follow show the progress that has taken place over the 60 years that the TRPS has run the TR.

Preservation in the strict meaning of the word was never possible. In 1951 the TR was in a very derelict state and by modern standards unsafe. Over the years the track has been relaid several times, the two original locomotives rebuilt, additional locomotives obtained and many additional coaches acquired. Facilities for its passengers and for the maintenance and storage of rolling stock have had to be built, and the character of the stations at Wharf, Pendre and Abergynolwyn has changed. However, the locomotive and carriages that opened the line to passengers in 1866 still run in regular service and much of the line through the valley of the Afon Fathew remains largely as built 145 years ago.

This collection of pictures commemorates the many men and women who have given of their time, skills and money over the past 60 years to ensure that the trains continue to run up the valley, bringing pleasure to the thousands who travel every year, as well as pleasure and satisfaction to those involved in the running, maintenance and administration of the TR. The Society has been fortunate in that members have often been involved for many years. There are still a good number of volunteers whose service goes back to the 1950s; for example, John Bate first came as a volunteer in July 1951 and, after a long stint as Chief Engineer, is still volunteering after retirement. After 60 years the TRPS is now being served by only its third Secretary and third Treasurer.

The pictures have been selected to show some of the major milestones during those 60 years. The Society took over a railway that was literally falling apart, and today it is a thriving railway, in fine condition yet with the original equipment still in daily use. Tom Rolt served as General Manager for the first two years and recorded the story of that early period in his book *Railway Adventure*. John Bate recorded the engineering side of the TRPS years in *The Chronicles of Pendre Sidings*, and Alan Holmes, another very long-standing volunteer, has dealt with the other aspects of the TRPS in *Talyllyn Revived*. The pictures are orientated towards work being done rather than pictures of trains.

With John Bate on the footplate and smoke from oily rags in the smokebox, the locomotive that was to become No 7 *Tom Rolt* is posed with volunteers. John Slater, for many years editor of the *Talyllyn News*, is on the right.

1. The 1950s: Early Days

Early discussions on how to save the Talyllyn Railway took place in the late 1940s at Bill Trinder's radio and record shop (now The Watch Workshop) in Banbury, which was also the location of Tom Rolt's narrow boat *Cressy*, upon which he was living.

A priority for the newly formed TRPS was additional motive power. Probably the only engines in the country to fit the TR track gauge and restricted loading gauge were the two remaining Corris Railway locomotives, which still lay at nearby Machynlleth following the closure of the CR in August 1948. Both were purchased from BR for £25 plus £12 10s carriage each, and were delivered to Tywyn in March 1951. The first 'new' locomotives in 85 years are seen on arrival at Wharf; numbered 3 and 4 on the CR, they retained those numbers on the TR and were named *Sir Haydn* and *Edward Thomas* respectively after the former owner and manager.

In the early 1950s there were a number of sorties up the mineral extension to recover rail. *Edward Thomas* waits at Forestry Crossing whilst the flange ways of the crossing have the accumulated mud and stone, which have washed down the track, dug out.

Volunteer working parties were envisaged from the formation of the TRPS and one of the first was held in March 1951 when track was lifted on the village incline at Abergynolwyn. In relatively good condition having only been used by wagons it would provide rails to patch the main line. The working party is seen at the Village Winding House. The party includes Owen Prosser (left) and Bill Faulkner (second right)

The 1950s: Early Days

The track along the mineral extension, east of Abergynolwyn station was in slightly better condition than the main line and the section beyond the Village Winding House was lifted in the early 1950s. Here the gang are track lifting on the loop, which went behind the Winding House, in what look like rather wet conditions.

The same train is seen at the Winding House. The decayed state of the lintel is obvious.

The Village incline working party lifting rail at the top of the incline.

On 12 May 1951 (Whit Saturday) a train was run to Abergynolwyn to deliver new station nameboards and other items; it is seen here at its destination.

14 May 1951: The First Public Train

The first public train was run at 10.00am on Monday 14 May 1951. Seen here is No 2 *Dolgoch* with the three Brown Marshall coaches and the brake-van at Wharf station. Tom Rolt is on the left and Bill Trinder, Chairman of the TRPS, stands behind the tape he will shortly cut to inaugurate the railway preservation era.

At Rhydyronen there was no run-round loop, so the carriages had to be pushed past the engine using the siding. Fortunately the trains were well loaded and there was no shortage of helpers. Here the train has been reversed for the return trip to Tywyn.

Later in the day the train was strengthened with the remaining carriage, built by Lancaster Wagon Co in 1867. There were five return trips, and here the heavy loading is obvious. In the centre of the group of spectators are Lady Haydn and Edward Thomas, the Manager of the railway under Sir Haydn.

Passengers disembark from one of the later trains on its return to Wharf. Bill Trinder (centre right) watches and no doubt feels satisfied the day has gone well. There was neither platform nor run-round loop at Wharf, running round being by gravity.

Thought to have been taken on 14 May, officials of the TRPS pose in front of *Dolgoch*. Left to right, they are David Curwen (Engineer), Bill Trinder (Chairman), Pat Whitehouse (Secretary), Tom Rolt (General Manager) and Pat Garland (Treasurer).

Later in the season, *Dolgoch*, now fitted with nameplates, runs through Pendre with a down train comprising all the coaches, with the ex-Corris Railway van at the rear. As well as the locomotives from the CR, the TRPS acquired the remaining serviceable wagons and the brake-van, this being donated by the person who had bought it for preservation.

In the summer of 1951 *Dolgoch* shunts the Corris van at Wharf with the entire passenger stock on the right. On the left, behind a couple of slate wagons, are the two ex-Corris Railway 2-ton coal wagons. The rails lying around are probably ones replaced by better rails from the Village incline.

Young admirers examine *Dolgoch* as it stands at Abergynolwyn after running round its train. The poor state of the track will be noted. *R. Sansbury*

Tom Rolt leans against carriage No 2 after the train has arrived at Abergynolwyn, talking to the TRPS Secretary, Pat Whitehouse, and his wife Thelma. Though there is evidence of carriage numbering in pre-Society days, no definitive list exists and the current numbers were allocated by the TRPS.

1952: The Second Season

At Easter 1952 *Dolgoch* heads out of Tywyn at Ty Mawr bridge on an empty ballast train; some of the gang are riding in the empty wagons. The train will proceed to Quarry Siding, where 'ballast' will be extracted from the small quarry there.

Digging ballast at Quarry. The ballast was actually shale, and tended to set like concrete. It certainly held the track in place, but lacked any drainage capability. Subsequently the TR used second-hand ballast from BR, and now uses new crushed stone. An ex-Corris wagon is being loaded. The siding was later realigned to give a longer working face.

A loaded ballast train stands at Quarry Siding on 13 April 1952. Some of the former CR wagons are still lettered 'GW'. On the main line stand an ex-CR wooden-bodied wagon and one of the 2-ton coal wagons.
J. N. Slater

A winter working party relays track at milepost 3 in December 1952. The sleepers on the right look to be the 'new' ones for the relay and are probably second-hand BR ones cut down.

1952: The Second Season

On 10 May 1952 a short works train comprising a slate wagon and the Corris van stands at Dolgoch. The gang looks anxiously at the locomotive *Dolgoch* as the injector has stuck, hence the cloud of steam. *J. N. Slater*

The following day *Dolgoch* has trouble with the water tank. The problem is not recorded, but it was probably leaking. The Corris van has been detached. This picture was taken from the quarry at Quarry Siding. *J. N. Slater*

The better of the two Corris Railway locomotives was No 3 *Sir Haydn*, but the combination of its narrow wheel treads and the appalling state of the track meant that it could not be safely used. No 4 *Edward Thomas* needed work on its firebox, and this was generously done by the Hunslet Engine Company of Leeds. The locomotive returned in time for the Whitsuntide opening in 1952, complete with a new saddle tank. Here it is awaiting unloading at Wharf, while the crane is being used to turn No 3 so that the single cab opening will be on the platform side. *Dolgoch* will haul the Corris engines back to Pendre.

On Whit Monday 1952 No 4 double-heads the morning train with *Dolgoch*. No 4's fire had been left banked up overnight and had clinkered, so she did not steam well – Tom Rolt describes the event in *Railway Adventure*. During the winter of 1951/52 a loop had been laid and a platform built.

1952: The Second Season

The track at Abergynolwyn was also relaid during that winter, and the improved track is seen here with *Dolgoch* and all the coaches on arrival in the summer of 1952.

Tom Rolt vividly describes 5 September 1952, the day when one of *Dolgoch*'s front springs failed while working the afternoon train. Here Tom peers at the engine as it pauses at Rhydyronen before making its cautious way to Pendre, where the train terminated, 29 minutes late.
G. Braithwaite

Edward Thomas hauls a works train at Rhydyronen in October 1952. Geoff Naylor is on the footplate and Bill Faulkner on the right. The train includes a genuine TR bolster and Corris chassis.

No 5 (1) stands in Pendre Works on Easter Monday 1953. John Bate records that the engine seized during the weekend and that is probably why the locomotive is in the works. *J. N. Slater*

The first internal-combustion locomotive on the TR was No 5, built by David Curwen and utilised the Ford Model T engine and epicyclic transmission from Tom Rolt's narrow boat *Cressy*. It is seen here on delivery to Wharf on 17 October 1952.

No 5 (1) is on its first run at Wharf, with Tom Rolt on the footplate. This locomotive had a short life; it was used to recover a failed *Edward Thomas*, which strained the engine and transmission, and it had been taken out of use by Easter 1953. The chassis still remains in use as a wagon. In the background are Tom's Alvis and David Curwen's Lea-Francis.

1953-1954

This undated picture, probably from 1954, shows *Edward Thomas* arriving at Abergynolwyn, with Pat Whitehouse as fireman. Refreshments, of a rather basic nature, were by now available. The former CR locomotives were not fitted with the TR side buffers until the mid-1950s; running plates were also fitted to *Edward Thomas* at the same time.

Edward Thomas stands at Pendre in 1953 or 1954, with Gareth Jones on the footplate and Bill Faulkner standing on the right. Bill was an early volunteer and served as a director of the company for many years, as well as being a regular driver.

Edward Thomas is seen again at Wharf with a train of original TR coaches. The locomotive is without TR buffers, again dating the picture to either 1953 or 1954.
The siding to the weighbridge, in front of the building, is still connected.

The first special headboard on a preserved railway was that carried on a special train for local schoolchildren to commemorate the Coronation in June 1953. Here Gareth Jones puts the headboard on *Edward Thomas*. Gareth joined British Railways at Machynlleth shed and went on to a successful career with BR.

Fifty years later another special was run to commemorate the Golden Jubilee of the Coronation, and Gareth returned to put the same headboard on the special, this time with *Talyllyn*, as *Edward Thomas* was undergoing a major rebuild.

During 1953 the Territorial Army worked on the track, and this assistance really helped the TR get on top of the track relaying, as increased traffic was wearing out the track faster than it could be repaired. Here the TA men are working on Dolgoch Viaduct – Health & Safety people nowadays would have heart attacks over some of the practices shown here!

Having said that, safety has always been paramount for the TRPS. Facing point locks had first been installed in June 1952, and one is shown here in the locked position, though with no padlock through the hasp. To open the point the padlock would be removed, the flap lifted and the tongue swung round, allowing the blade to move.
J. N. Slater

The Annual General Meeting of the TRPS is held in Tywyn at the end of September each year, and in 1953 a special train was run from London for members to attend. Leaving Paddington early on the Saturday morning, arrival in Tywyn about lunch time gave members time to travel on the TR before the evening meeting and an overnight return journey. Ex-GWR railcar No W13W ran the first trip, and the driver is looking at the engine while standing at Welshpool on the outward journey; the railcar failed through loss of cooling water at Lapworth on the return.

Many members not only worked on the railway but also did various 'behind-the-scenes' tasks at home. John Slater was an early member and for many years produced a newsletter after each of his visits; these provide an invaluable record of volunteer activity. John later became the editor of the quarterly TRPS magazine, *Talyllyn News. J. N. Slater*

Publicity has been important for the TRPS since its foundation. This was helped by a number of models of the railway, and here a 7mm-scale model of Pendre is on display at the Model Railway Club's exhibition in London in 1953. The layout is being admired by Pat Garland, Robby Robertson, who organised the AGM specials for many years, and J. J. Davis, who was a guard and also a keen photographer, many of whose pictures are in the collection. *J. H. L. Adams*

A 4mm-scale model of Dolgoch station and viaduct was also built in the mid-1950s. A very early example of narrow-gauge modelling in this scale, the motor was in the brake-van and the layout was automatically operated. It was known as 'The Aquarium' and is now preserved at Wharf in working order.

With Bill Faulkner on the footplate, *Edward Thomas* stands at Abergynolwyn in 1953, while John Snell looks on. John was fireman on the first train in 1951 and went on to manage the Romney, Hythe & Dymchurch Railway.

Edward Thomas is seen again on arrival at Abergynolwyn. During the 1950s some trains only stopped at Dolgoch and Abergynolwyn, but here the carriage board identifies an all-stations service. Unusually the brake-van is at the east (uphill) end of the train, though it is certain there will be another braked vehicle at the back.

Colour pictures of the TR in early TRPS days are uncommon. Here *Edward Thomas* stands at Wharf station in 1954, coupled to the TR van. The engine is still without TR buffing gear and running plates, and headlamps did not seem to be used in the early Society days.

An appeal for funds to businesses in the Midlands resulted in the offer of a locomotive by Abelson & Co. A 2-foot-gauge 0-4-0 well tank built by Andrew Barclay in 1918 for the Admiralty Air Service Construction Corps, it had last worked at RAF Calshot in 1945. In April 1953 it was handed over by Mr Douglas Abelson, in the centre and after whom the engine was to be named, to the TRPS President, the Earl of Northesk, with the nameplate. *J. H. L. Adams*

Douglas was then loaded on to a low-loader to be taken to Hunt Bros' works at Oldbury for regauging and modifications to the cab and brake. *J. H. L. Adams*

On the Pickfords low-loader, with the BR crest on the side and with speed limited to 20mph, *Douglas* prepares to leave Abelson's works. *J. H. L. Adams*

Douglas stands with a train at Wharf, in a view showing the layout as altered in the winter of 1951/52. The short train comprises coach No 9, a six-compartment bogie vehicle built at Pendre in 1955 on a bogie chassis from W. G. Allen, which had run the previous season with two open bodies from the Penrhyn Quarry Railway, and the TR van brings up the rear.

A view of carriage No 9 under construction in Pendre Works. Built with softwood and hardboard, the panels warped and the body was condemned and replaced by a Tisdale-built hardwood five-compartment body for the 1968 season. *J. N. Slater*

Some 40 years later *Douglas* is seen running on the TR in standard livery. It was fitted with a new boiler in 1995 and is currently undergoing a major overhaul.

After the new boiler was fitted *Douglas* was hastily painted in a camouflage livery to appear in an event for the 50th anniversary of end of the Second World War. The livery is entirely fictional.

Douglas was slightly higher than the TR locomotives and the track under the skew arch bridge at the top of Hendy bank had to be lowered, involving breaking away the solid rock. The limited clearance is obvious.

Douglas spent the winter of 1995/96 at the RAF Museum in Hendon alongside a Lancaster bomber. It was painted in what is thought to have been the livery in which it was delivered in 1918, although then it had a large brass plate reading 'AIRSERVICE CONSTRUCTIONAL CORPS No 1'.

No 3 *Sir Haydn* in seen in Pendre loco shed on 6 April 1953. The door to the workshop is to the right of the engine. This was the first year that *Sir Haydn* was able to run in service, as the track had been improved. *J. N. Slater*

Sir Haydn heads along the grass-grown track towards Abergynolwyn in 1953.

The limited number of coaches quickly became a problem as passenger numbers increased. The three-compartment open coaches used on the Penrhyn Quarry Railway's quarrymen's trains had been out of use since the service ceased in February 1951, and were owned by the Workman's Train Society; that body was defunct by 1953, which complicated the acquisition of some of the coaches.

The first two bodies, H and P, were donated, and a further four – C, D, E and G – were then purchased. Here body E is being offloaded at Wharf by (left to right) John Slater, John Bate and Chips Harrison.

The body of Penrhyn E is manoeuvred off the BR wagon on which it has arrived on to a TR flat wagon. E never ran on the TR, but parts of it were used in carriage No 10.

Sir Haydn stands at Wharf on a wet day. The leading carriage is No 10, built on the second Allen chassis and having a five-compartment open body and a guard's compartment. The body was built at Pendre and incorporated parts of some of the Penrhyn bodies; it entering service in June 1954.

Sir Haydn runs into Wharf station, probably in early 1954 as buffers have not been fitted. The shed on the right was built in the first years of the 1900s and is usually referred to as the gunpowder shed, though its exact usage is unclear. In TRPS days it became the first museum and is now the museum store.

Sir Haydn runs round at Wharf, probably in the summer of 1954, as buffers have been fitted to the locomotive but the bridge has not been rebuilt. The buffer stop looks to have been hit hard. The rails on the right are probably from Nuneaton.

No 3 *Sir Haydn* only had a cab opening on the right-hand side and was turned to work cab-first up the line. It is seen here on arrival at Abergynolwyn some time after August 1954, when the TR side buffers were fitted. The boiler was in poor condition and it was withdrawn in 1958, returning to service with a new boiler in 1968 after a major rebuild at Pendre.

John Slater's note on the rear of this print reads, 'Special fast train setting back at Pendre to collect its brake-van, which had become detached. 25th September 1954'. It was the day of the AGM and the train would be a special for members who had arrived on the AGM special, which that year was a two-car GWR diesel unit, Nos W33W and W38W, with an extra coach in the centre. What had happened at Pendre is not recorded. The last coach is No 9, with the two Penrhyn bodies.

A second internal-combustion locomotive arrived in 1954. Numbered 7, it was a Mercury yard tractor converted to run on rails, with a four-wheel bogie replacing the front axle. It was donated by Major Walker of Cheltenham, and here his lorry is delivering the locomotive to Wharf.

No 7 was later fitted with a roof and it is seen here at Quarry Siding. It did useful work, though it lacked adhesion, and was only withdrawn from use when the Ruston diesel arrived in March 1957.

The one serious problem with No 7 was that it only had one, very slow, reverse gear, and therefore had to be turned at the end of each trip. It was lifted on a jack and swung round, as is happening here at Quarry Siding.

Later, No 7 is on a short works train at Rhydyronen, probably in the winter of 1955/56, when the loop was being reinstated. The weed-killing wagon is at the rear. Geoff Naylor is driving and Jim Lloyd is on the front. Jim's maps and drawings were used in many of James Boyd's books.

A London Area working party unloads scrap sleepers at Pendre on 30 October 1954. No 7 is standing on the main line with a mixed collection of wagons, the TR van and No 6. The Penrhyn bodies on the left are C and D, which had been mounted on the bogie chassis as No 9 for the 1954 season. *J. N. Slater*

On Easter Sunday 1954 a gang unloads cast-iron scrap at Wharf. It is mainly old chairs that have been pulled out during the military relaying of the previous year. The original TR track was a mixture of chairs and spikes. *J. N. Slater*

The low winter sunshine glints on *Edward Thomas* and the Corris van at Abergynolwyn in 1954, while working an engineering train.

1955

During the winter of 1954/55 a weed-killing wagon was built by the North West Area group. It is seen outside Pendre shed with James Boyd, a well-known author on narrow-gauge railways, sitting on the tanks, which display the sense of humour that still exists on the TR.

In March 1955 the weed-killing wagon is being tested, propelled by the motor trolley; Geoff Naylor is in the 'footplate'. The weed-killer was spread by gravity from the tanks through the spray bar.

During that same winter the Aberdovey road, which crosses Wharf bridge, was widened and the bridge renewed. Some railway land was needed for the widening and the new retaining wall can be seen in the foreground, while the older bridge is still in place.

This track-level view shows the retaining wall being built before the new bridge was erected. The wall along the road has been demolished and the south-side retaining wall is going up.

Work was also done on the east side of the bridge, with spoil being removed in TR wagons. The motor trolley, built by John Bate and newly arrived, is on the extreme right.

In March 1955 *Edward Thomas* is undergoing a major overhaul in Pendre Works. During this overhaul new buffer beams were fitted, as was TR buffing gear. The primitive conditions in the works are obvious.

Two trains stand at Wharf in May 1955, probably during the Whitsuntide holiday. *Sir Haydn*'s train on the right includes a Brown Marshall coach and bogie carriage No 9, while *Douglas*, on the left, has the other three TR coaches and a Penrhyn open. The recently rebuilt Wharf bridge is in the background. *J. H. L. Adams*

On 30 May the piles of sleepers seen the previous year (see page 39) are still in evidence at Pendre as No 6 passes with an up train with the rebodied carriage No 9 as leading vehicle. On the right is a barn originally used for storing hay collected from the lineside, and in which the out-of-use *Talyllyn* stood in early TRPS days. *J. N. Slater*

On 28 May 1955 *Sir Haydn*, on an Abergynolwyn-bound train and driven by Dai Jones, climbs Cynfal Bank past a gang who are hedging and weeding. The overgrown state of the track is evident. *J. N. Slater*

Photographed from Cynfal bridge, a loaded ballast train descends Cynfal Bank on 31 July 1955. The gang are riding in a Penrhyn open, and the locomotive is recorded as *Sir Haydn*. *J. N. Slater*

1956-1960

John Slater recorded this afternoon down train on Whit Sunday, 20 May 1956, as having had 285 passengers, probably a record – it must have been very cramped. The train comprises four TR coaches, two opens and the two bogie coaches, Nos 9 and 10. The loco is *Edward Thomas*.

In this undated picture, probably about 1956, *Douglas* passes Quarry Siding points with a Tywyn-bound train.

In the 1950s the track was relaid and patched with a variety of second-hand rail. The need to acquire better rail was vital, and the TR found suitable sources in various quarries that were closing their railway systems. The TR contracted to lift and remove the rail from Jee's Quarry at Nuneaton, and here a gang is at work. *L. Bedder*

A Land Rover is used to pull out rails on the Jee's Quarry line. *L. Bedder*

Jee's Quarry rail is loaded for transportation to Tywyn. Much of it was unusable and was sold for scrap. *L. Bedder*

Joining the different sections of original and replacement rail was a problem until Pendre Works acquired a milling machine that enabled proper junction plates to be made, ensuring smooth joints. Correct-section fishplates are vital to maintaining level track joints, and John Slater machined many hundreds over the years.

A few years later the TRPS was also contracted to lift the Crich Mineral Railway in Derbyshire. The main-line rail between Crich Quarry and Ambergate was generally usable on the TR, but the track in the quarry area was mostly sold as scrap. A gang of volunteers lifts track along the main line. *R. K. Walton*

John Bate's Land Rover was used to pull out the rails in the Crich quarry area. Through links between some TRPS members and the Tramway Museum Society, the latter subsequently became aware of the site, which is now the National Tramway Museum. *J. N. Slater*

Increasing traffic led to the search for further carriages that would fit the TR's restricted loading gauge. The former 1st Class carriage from the Glyn Valley Tramway was purchased in 1956 from a garden in Chirk and taken to Tywyn for restoration. A second body, one of the 3rd Class coaches, was located at a farm near Glyn Ceiriog in 1958, and also purchased. It is seen here as found; Bill Faulkner (right) is examining it with John Wilkins, a Midlands industrialist and then the owner of the Fairbourne Railway. Mr Wilkins gave a great deal of support to the TR in the early days, being a director for a short while and providing practical assistance with materials, manpower from the FR, and funding.

This is the GVT 1st Class carriage as it arrived at Tywyn in January 1957, awaiting transportation to Pendre. It was taken up the line on a pair of cut-down slate wagons and was a very tight clearance through the bridges.

The GVT 1st Class carriage is being rebuilt in Pendre Works. The bodywork was largely carried out by 'the Greens', a father and son team. Mr Green Snr had been an apprentice in the Cambrian Railways' carriage shops at Oswestry.

The rebuilt GVT coaches are seen again when newly in service in 1958. Both were restored as 1st Class carriages, becoming TR Nos 14 and 15. This coach had been overhauled commercially in the Midlands and received the ornate lining once carried on the GVT. *J. N. Slater*

Another coach was found as a summer house near Gobowen, and the body was purchased by the TR in 1958. Corris Railway No 8 was the last new coach purchased by the CR, and when the line's passenger service ended on 31 December 1930 it was taken to Oswestry and subsequently sold to a GWR employee. Here it is being prepared for removal by a working party on 12 April 1959. *R. K. Walton*

Removing the coach body was not easy, as the trees in the orchard had to be navigated. It was rolled on a track of old sleepers.

After being rolled out into a meadow the body was loaded on to a BR trailer. The plan was to take it by rail, but in the event it went all the way by road and the overhang damaged the already corroded underframe.

The body was in a worse condition than expected, and only some parts were used in the rebuild. The finished coach, with new underframe and bogies, stands at Pendre with 'the Greens', who did the rebuild, on the right and Don Gardiner, who did work on the underframe and bogies, on the left. It entered service as TR No 17 in 1961 and carries Corris Railway livery of brown with gold lining.

Covered accommodation for the carriages was essential, and the original carriage shed at Pendre only held the four TR coaches and the van. In 1957 it was agreed to build a two-road shed on the north side of the line at Pendre, where the barn stood; some additional land was also purchased. The roof trusses of the old cutting shed at Fron Goch (between Aberdovey and Pennal), which belonged to the Haydn Jones estate, were purchased and dismantled for transportation to Pendre. Here in October 1957 the gang prepare to remove the trusses, with Richard Hope, Secretary for many years and now President, supervising on the left..

The trusses are raised on to the steel stanchions on 26 May 1958 as the shed, now known as the North Carriage Shed, takes shape.

During the winter of 1962/63 the North Carriage Shed was extended to provide further covered accommodation for the growing fleet of carriages. The end panels of the 1958 building were removed for the extension, the stanchions of which are seen here in place, with the roof trusses lying on the ground.

The North Shed was clad with asbestos cement sheeting, and here John Slater is fastening the upper panels on the lean-to extension that was built on the south side as engineering stores.

The 1867-built shed and works had a slate-roofed wooden carriage shed extending west along the centre road, and over the years the weight of the roof had caused the sides to splay. In 1960 it was decided to replace the building before it fell down. Here most of the shed has been demolished and the steel stanchions and roof trusses lie on the ground. Pendre station is to the left of the loco shed. *J. N. Slater*

The steelwork goes up. The rebuilt structure maintains the style of the earlier shed, but has been bricked up to the level of the side timbers, whereas the old shed was open at the bottom. *J. N. Slater*

1956-1960

Sir Haydn awaits departure from Abergynolwyn in 1957. The driver, standing next to the cab, is Herbert Jones, who, with his brother Dai and father Hugh, had worked on the railway in pre-Society days.

The TRPS President, the Earl of Northesk, makes a presentation to Herbert Jones at the 1957 AGM. *J. H. L. Adams*

In June 1958 *Edward Thomas* became derailed while entering the siding at Rhydyronen due to a loose check rail. Here it is being levered back onto track using a fulcrum of sleepers and a rail. Herbert Jones is positioning the rail.

After using diesel railcars for the AGM special trains in 1953 and 1954, steam-hauled trains were run until 1966. Unusual locomotives were used, and here ex-SECR Wainwright 'D' Class 4-4-0 No 31075 waits to leave Tywyn on the overnight journey back to London. The train was double-headed with ex-GWR 'Dean Goods' No 2538 as far as Shrewsbury, where 'Star' Class No 4065 took over for the run to Paddington, routed via Stratford, Kingham, Oxford and Thame due to weekend engineering work. Members staying in Tywyn would gather at the station to watch the train depart. *J. H. L. Adams*

No 1 *Talyllyn* had lain out of use since the mid-1940s and, although *Dolgoch* had been taken to the Midlands for rebuilding in 1954, little had been done. Eric Gibbons, a Midland Area member, offered to have No 1 rebuilt at his engineering works at Lenches Bridge, so *Talyllyn* departed on 24 March 1957 on the low-loader that had delivered Ruston diesel No 5. *Douglas* did the shunting and can be seen on the left.

A very sorry-looking *Talyllyn* stands in Gibbons Bros works before rebuilding starts. *J. H. L. Adams*

The rebuilt *Talyllyn* leaves Gibbons Bros in June 1958. It was almost a new locomotive, but was an unreliable performer until a major overhaul in the late 1960s sorted out a lot of problems, since when it has performed well. *J. H. L. Adams*

Left: One of the more unusual locomotives used on an AGM special was former Lancashire & Yorkshire Railway 2-4-2 radial tank No 50781, which piloted 'Dukedog' No 9021 from Shrewsbury to Tywyn on 28 September 1957. They are seen here at Welshpool, but No 50781 was failed at Machynlleth shed.

Young boys admire the rebuilt *Talyllyn* on its arrival at Wharf on 14 June 1958, before being offloaded. This is one of the very few pictures showing the rear of the station building. The new museum building is going up in the background.
J. H. L. Adams

Talyllyn is seen on an early run at Dolgoch. Tom Rolt is to the right of the locomotive.

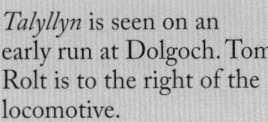

The embankment over a culvert at the west end of Dolgoch woods had given trouble over the years, and in late 1954 a low retaining wall had been built to support the track. Here a working party is working on that wall.

The first job was to locate the south end of the culvert and clear it out to drain the pond that had formed south of the line, then to slew the track southwards away from the edge of the slip. A concrete retaining was then built at the foot of the embankment. This involved first driving in old rails using a pile driver borrowed from the River Board. Here the pile driver is being erected in early 1958.

In November 1957 a more serious slip occurred, surveyed here by Richard Hope and Bill Faulkner. They had accompanied John Bate to assess the damage and for John to work out a plan to both restore the line for traffic and to devise a plan to solve the problem, which had been caused by a blocked culvert. *J. L. H. Bate*

After the rails had been driven in, shuttering was erected round them and concrete mixed at rail level was shot down a chute on scaffolding to be placed within the shuttering.

The retaining wall rises. The rectangular hole at the bottom is for the culvert pipe, which will be installed later.

After the retaining wall was built some 200 tons of shale from the quarry had to be tipped to rebuild the embankment. John Bate purchased four tipper bodies, which were mounted on TR wagon frames. Here John (second from left) watches as another load is tipped.

The last part of the slip repair, in early 1960, was to open up a trench to reveal the old culvert, made of slate slabs, and replace it with a concrete pipe. This involved timbering the sides of the trench and carrying the track over the trench on heavy timbers.

Finally the trench was filled in and the job was done. Nowadays the site is barely visible and the younger members have no recollection of the two years' hard labour that went into repairing the slip.

The other end of the filling process at the slip was digging and loading the shale at the quarry, and here a gang are loading wagons. Two gangs worked loading the shale into wheelbarrows, which were then tipped into wagons. In this case open wagons are being loaded for use as ballast. The wagon on the right is one of the 2-ton Corris vehicles, known as 'Queen Marys', which took more effort to unload at site. John Halliday, wheeling the barrow, acquired the title of 'Brutal Quarry Master' while leading the gangs at the quarry, a title that is still used by the outdoor foreman as a mark of pride.

To ease the work of loading Gibbons Bros provided a conveyor and hopper. Though good in theory, the shale would not slide down inside the hopper and if left in it for any time tended to set solid. Someone can be seen in the hopper pushing the material down to the opening.

This is Wharf station at Easter 1960. *Edward Thomas*, now fitted with the Giesl ejector chimney, heads a mixed rake, with a TR coach followed by one of the Glyn Valley coaches, three opens and the two bogie coaches, Nos 9 and 10. Lord Northesk stands in front of *Edward Thomas*, while a queue is waiting to book tickets at the office. Work has just started on the siding being installed for storing spare carriages, but usually used for wagons. The new museum building is in the background.

The largest exhibit in the museum was *Cambrai*, an 0-6-0T metre-gauge locomotive, originally from France and latterly working at Loddington ironstone mine near Kettering. Offloaded near the former gunpowder store in December 1960, it is being moved over temporary track to the new museum building in March 1961.

2. The 1960s: Expansion and Consolidation

The loop at Wharf is restricted in length by the site being squeezed between the standard-gauge railway and the road bridge. Here *Edward Thomas* is pole-shunting the train to clear the east-end points and regain the front of the train. The fireman holds the pole while Bill Faulkner eases up. The locomotive is carrying the limited-stop train headboard.

In the very cold winter of 1962/3 the water supply to Pendre froze, and was thawed using the arc welder connected to the stop-cock in the street. Not necessarily conventional, but effective!

The 1960s: Expansion and Consolidation

The growing traffic of the 1960s made the provision of yet more coaches essential, and a six-compartment coach, based on the style of the Glyn Valley coaches, was designed. 'The Greens' built the bodywork and the underframe and bogies were built at Pendre. Here the Greens are assembling the body; they prepared many of the components at home and brought them to Tywyn for assembly.

The completed body, in primer in the North Carriage Shed, awaits mounting on the bogies.

The bogies were basically a half-size copy of LMS examples, but the suspension caused the coach to roll badly in service and dampers had to be fitted. Here Alan Meaden pushes one of the bogies through Pendre yard.

The finished coach stands at Pendre. Though a beautiful piece of craftsmanship, it had taken nearly five years to build, and to ensure enough coaches for the growing traffic future vehicles were built commercially.

The 1960s: Expansion and Consolidation

The TRPS gradually extended a telephone line up the railway. Phil Glazebrook, a GPO engineer from London, did much work on the line over many years.

Maintaining the railway's property is an ongoing task. The southern side of the cutting west of Pendre bridge gave trouble through water ingress and a retaining wall was put in, supported by old rails attached to frames set in concrete and with a support going under the rails. Here the Yorkshire Area gang is erecting the rail supports and inserting slate slabs behind them in the winter of 1965.

When built in 1867 Pendre shed and works were at the edge of the town and surrounded by fields, but during the 1960s the town expanded and houses were built on the land to the south of the site. A high fence was erected along the boundary, using old rails set in concrete as uprights. John Halliday wheels a barrow-load of concrete up to a post-hole with assistance from Neal Chapman.

The use of the little office in Abergynolwyn station for the sale of refreshments was not satisfactory, and John Bate suggested the use of a mobile 'tea van'; this was built on the chassis of Penrhyn open No 7 and went into use in the summer of 1963, with opening flaps on the south side for serving. In 1963 it stood against a temporary timber platform beyond the east points and is seen here from the rear as *Douglas* shunts it into place.

The 1960s: Expansion and Consolidation

For the 1964 and subsequent seasons the 'tea van' stood on a short siding at the east end of the station, adjacent to the building, and during Easter 1964 the ground is being excavated for the siding. The water supply to the station ran along the site of the siding and care was required not to puncture it. *Dolgoch* had returned to traffic in mid-1963, and the first coach is the Corris carriage.

The 'tea van' was brought up at the front of the first train of the day, then shunted into the siding, here by *Douglas*. The van remained in use until the end of the 1968 season, after which the station was rebuilt with a proper refreshment room.

THE TALYLLYN RAILWAY 60 Years of Preservation

The TR is responsible for the maintenance of the hedges and fences along each side of the line, some 14 miles in all. To aid hedge-cutting a Bomford 'Hedgemaker' cutter was acquired and mounted on an ex-Ffestiniog wagon. The original petrol engine proved inconvenient and was replaced by an electric motor, as seen here, powered by a generator on the train. Used with locomotive No 8, which had a hydrostatic transmission and could be driven at very slow speeds, it proved useful until replaced by the flail-mower. The rebuilt south shed is on the left.

At the foot of the two inclines that led to the quarry at Bryneglwys lay a number of wrecked wagons, no doubt the result of some mishap on the incline. Over the years the wheels, etc, have been recovered for further use. Some wheels had ended up in the waters of the Gwernol and required diving to attach ropes for recovery. Here a couple of derelict slate wagons are at the foot of the Cantrybedd incline.

The TR was always on the look-out for items that would be useful. The demolition of property at Ynysymaengwyn, the former home of the Corbett family and now a caravan site, made a water tank available and a gang duly removed it – no doubt quite a challenge. It was used with the Pendre water column.

The well-known railway and wildlife painter Terence Cuneo painted two pictures of the TR in the 1960s. The first featured *Talyllyn* leaving Dolgoch, and the preliminary sketches of the locomotive were done at Brynglas. Although Dai Jones is posing for the artist he does not appear in the finished picture.

The second Cuneo picture depicted *Dolgoch* on Dolgoch Viaduct, and here the artist sketches the scene while sitting on the edge of the ravine.

1964-1965: Redeveloping Wharf

The facilities at Wharf, having been designed for slate traffic, were not really satisfactory for the growing number of passengers, so the layout was revised in the winter of 1964/65 with the building extended and a platform created in front of it. Before this was done the weighbridge had to be removed. Here the frame has been lifted out and is about to be railed away to storage in September 1964. There have been various plans to reinstate the weighbridge elsewhere at Wharf, and these should finally be achieved later in 2011.

By December 1964 the only remaining track was the 1960-installed siding that had been diverted at the west end to provide access to the wharf edge siding, previously accessed by turntables.

1964-1965: Redeveloping Wharf

During the winter the new layout began to take shape, and here the new platform is being formed in front of the building. *Cambrai* is standing alongside the museum.

Looking east along the site, the gang is building the platform wall.

A temporary track has been laid to clear spoil from the rear of the station building so that an extension can be built. On the left the museum building is being extended. The toilet block by the station entrance was built and operated by Tywyn Council. On the right Mike Hynd and Colin Roobottom are installing the ground frame.

The new track layout is in place, the building extension is going up and the flat roof is being put on. The platform has been back-filled and is being compacted. The blocks on the extreme left are for the museum extension.

The finished station: the new layout is installed and ballasted, the awning is being completed, the garden area is being tidied up and fenced. The 'shrubbery' would later be occupied by temporary structures and finally a new toilet block.

The north side of the redeveloped station had display windows in the new extension. The boulder on the left will protect the awning from vehicles entering the yard. The boulder is reputed to have come from Bryneglwys in response to a local lady requesting some rockery stone; however, she never took delivery and it still protects the building.

Inside the original building the space was opened up to provide a sales area by removing the wall between the two rooms. The chimney breast would be removed in a later alteration.

1965: The Centenary

The centenary of the Act incorporating the Talyllyn Railway was commemorated in 1965 and a number of special celebration events took place. A named train, 'The Centenarian', was run throughout the season, and here the inaugural train stands at Abergynolwyn on 1 June 1965 with John Betjeman alongside in the black raincoat.

On 21 February *Talyllyn* was loaded up for transport to Birmingham where it was displayed as part of the centenary celebrations. No 5 *Midlander*, a Ruston diesel obtained from Jee's Quarry and regauged from 2ft 6½in in the Midlands before coming to Tywyn in 1957, shunts *Talyllyn* carefully over a temporary track on to the low loader. The platform and building extensions are under way.

The Vintage Sports Car Club, another of Tom Rolt's interests, had a rally to Tywyn and here cars are seen arriving at Wharf station.

The Merioneth County Show was held in the fields at Hendy, and a shuttle service was provided from Wharf to Hendy Halt. Comprising the Corris coach and van, the train was topped and tailed by *Dolgoch* and *Talyllyn*, and is seen at Pendre waiting for a service train to pass. David Room is the guard, standing by *Talyllyn*.

A historical exhibition commemorating the centenary of the TR was staged in the hall of Tywyn School. One exhibit was a wagon, which was towed to the school by John Bate's Land Rover and is seen here leaving Wharf along the main road. The Land Rover is still going strong.

1965: The Centenary

In August 1965 Brynglas loop was fitted with a ground frame to operate the points, and the frame is seen here as first installed with very basic facilities for the operator.

By 1966 the last of the Penrhyn opens in service was No 8, which had been used on works trains and was in very poor condition. Here the author assists in its scrapping on the Wharf edge siding. Behind are two of the hopper wagons from Winchburgh shale quarry in Scotland.

The major engineering work on the line is Dolgoch Viaduct. By 1968 the spandrel walls were distorting, probably due to blocked drains. A temporary solution in May was to fit tie-bars, which involved digging trenches across the viaduct and drilling holes through the walls. A frame on the viaduct held wooden pads against the outside of the walls to prevent the bricks from being pushed outwards during drilling.

The wooden frame is moved along the viaduct to drill the next holes.

1965: The Centenary

After the holes were drilled, bars with threaded ends were pushed through. The bars were connected inside the walls with a turnbuckle, and metal plates with nuts welded on were put on the outside. Getting these plates started on the thread was not easy. A loop was welded to the plate and a rope looped through to prevent the plate dropping into the ravine. Here Roger Freeman locates the plate on the bar while Colin Roobottom holds the rope.

Now it is Ian Howitt's job to fit a plate. When the turnbuckles were tightened the mortar squeezed out of the brickwork like toothpaste.

With the tie-bars and plates in place the trenches were backfilled and the track replaced. The tie-bars were only a temporary expedient, and the spandrel walls were rebuilt by Buttington Contractors during the winter of 1969/70.

Prior to the 1967 and 1968 seasons respectively carriages Nos 9 and 10 had been fitted with new hardwood bodies manufactured by Raymond Tisdale of Kenilworth, and those bodies formed the basis for new coaches built by Tisdale on underframes manufactured by Midland Furnace Co. The first to arrive was No 19, a six-compartment 1st/3rd Composite. The bogies were manufactured at Pendre, and the body shells were fitted out and painted there. Here No 19, on temporary bogies, is pulled out of the north shed by *Midlander*, driven by TRPS Treasurer Colin Roobottom, in April 1968.

3. 1968-69: Rebuilding Abergynolwyn

Abergynolwyn station was rebuilt during the winter of 1968/69 to provide better passenger facilities. It was intended to use the slate from the Village Winding House, which was in poor condition and would have to be demolished when the passenger service was extended to Nant Gwernol. This meant taking trains along the mineral extension east of Abergynolwyn, which had lain disused since sorties there in the 1950s, and involved clearing overhanging branches and making the track usable. Here a tree is cut back while *Midlander* and the TR van wait.

This view shows the west-end points with the Village Winding House in the background. Access to the incline tracks was from a wagon turntable in the loop running behind the building.

The Village Winding House looking west: the rotten lintel is obvious, as is the cracked walling. The track to the top of the incline passes through the building left to right.

This is the interior of the winding house after the roof had been removed. The drum is still in place and volunteers start to demolish the walls.

Looking west from the top of the winding house, *Midlander* is standing on the main line and the Corris van is on the short stub that was all that remained of the loop round the back of the building.

With the gables demolished there just remain the four pillars that formed the base of the winding house; the winding drum has been dropped to the ground. The photograph was taken from the top of the incline, and one of the bent rails that went over the edge is visible in the bottom left-hand corner. The pedestal on the right carried the brake lever used to control wagon speed on the incline.

1968-1969: Rebuilding Abergynolwyn

In September 1968 the slate shelter at Abergynolwyn station was demolished so that the new station building could be constructed by contractors over the winter. The shelter had been built in about 1939 to replace the original wooden building, which had succumbed to wind and weather.

A notice showing photographs of the architect's model of the new station building was erected to explain to passengers what was going on.

TRPS secretary Richard Hope enjoys a little light demolition with a 14lb hammer; he specifically asked that the sink be saved for him.

The site has been cleared and potentially useful slate blocks piled up for use by the contractors. Although it had been hoped to use slate from the winding house, it was of poor quality and only useful for foundation filling. Better-quality block was obtained from derelict buildings at Bryneglwys Quarry.

During the winter the new building took shape, despite the weather not always being helpful. In the background *Midlander* has brought an engineering train with materials.

The view from the west shows the works train and the new building.

1968-1969: Rebuilding Abergynolwyn

During the week before Easter a steam works train has arrived at Abergynolwyn. The building is nearer to completion, but would not be opened before the 1969 season started.

One of the Easter service trains arrives at the unfinished station. *Sir Haydn* has been rebuilt at Pendre and this is one of its first workings. It now faces uphill and has been fitted with a new cab to give greater headroom and access from both sides.

During Easter 1969 preparations were also in hand for laying a loop at Quarry Siding in readiness for the three-train peak service. *Douglas* and *Edward Thomas* double-head a works train shunting at Quarry; the Corris van had been fitted with a new body in 1958 and the former body was used as a shelter at Quarry, placed to the right of the points.

A general view of the quarry with the gang barrowing shale into wagons.

Old sleepers were used as a retaining wall to hold the quarry floor above the siding. Charlie Daniel hammers in a rail to hold up the wall.

The planned three-train peak service not only required a loop at Quarry Siding, and the upgrading of Pendre loop to enable passenger trains to cross there, but also needed at least three engines to be steamed daily during the peak, and the locomotive shed at Pendre only held two. Beyond the shed was the cottage provided for Mr Bousted, who came with the engines from Fletcher Jennings in the 1860s. It had been occupied by TR employees ever since and latterly by Herbert Jones, the Locomotive Superintendent. He vacated the cottage and the locomotive shed was extended so that it could hold four locomotives. In this October 1968 view the intervening wall has been demolished and *Dolgoch* peers into the house. Electrical trunking, formerly on the wall, is suspended temporarily from the roof.

Temporary track was laid into the cottage and in due course a pit was dug and the floor level lowered to make it easier to work on locomotives that would receive some overhaul work in this end of the shed in the winter.

Sir Haydn had been withdrawn from service in 1958, needing a new boiler, which was ordered from J. & W. Gower of Bedford in 1964. A couple of years later the locomotive was taken into Pendre Works for an extensive rebuild, the first time such work had been undertaken there. The new boiler is on the frames and the redesigned cab lies on a wagon on the right. TRPS Treasurer Colin Roobottom stands, hammer in hand, alongside.

Locomotive Developments

With the new design of cab fitted, giving greater headroom, *Sir Haydn* is nearing completion in Pendre Works. It still awaits the saddle tank. The forge is in the centre at the rear.

Now in white primer, the rebuild is nearing completion. The saddle tank has been fitted and the locomotive is being piped up.

In October 1968 *Sir Haydn* is steamed for its first outing and coupled onto the rear of the last down service train at Pendre for a trip to Wharf. On the left John Adams, a professional photographer, whose TR pictures are now in the TR collection and have been used in this book, records the scene on his cine-camera.

Locomotive Developments

At Easter 1969 *Sir Haydn*, now in TR green livery, heads a train away from Quarry Siding on its way to Abergynolwyn; the locomotive has been in regular service ever since. A new firebox was fitted in 1991, but the 1964 boiler is now nearing the end of its life and serious boiler work will be required in 2012

One aspect of the TRPS that is not often photographed is the many committees that constitute the way the society is run. Photographer John Adams has caught the Engineering Committee holding an alfresco meeting on the platform at Wharf station. The committee structure is an integral part of the TRPS's very democratic constitution, and while it can at times be cumbersome it does involve the membership in the running of the railway.

In the 1960s traffic was expanding and the need was felt for more powerful locomotives. Various schemes were considered. In January 1969 the TR was able to purchase a 3-foot-gauge 0-4-0 tank that had been built in 1948 for the Irish Turf Board, intended to burn turf. It had not been successful and the engine had done little work. However, it would provide the TR with a 'kit of parts' from which to build a locomotive at Pendre. On arrival at Wharf in March 1969 it was soon informally named 'Irish Pete'.

John Bate designed an 0-4-2 side tank utilising the wheels, cylinders and boiler of the original engine. New frames were built at Pendre and, with the cylinders attached, the frames have been wheeled out to be photographed with the volunteers who had worked on the project. John Bate is fourth from the right.

Locomotive Developments

Later the boiler was placed on the frames and photographed in the yard at Pendre. *Edward Thomas* is standing in the station with a down train. With traffic dropping off in the 1970s and with improved performance by *Talyllyn* and *Dolgoch*, work on No 7 was suspended. However, with *Douglas*'s boiler nearing the end of its life, work resumed in 1988, and No 7 entered service in 1991.

Here is No 7 as completed, and named *Tom Rolt* in honour of the TR pioneer. More massive in appearance than the other engines, it has performed well and takes it turns on the roster. It is seen here at Nant Gwernol.

THE TALYLLYN RAILWAY 60 Years of Preservation

The boiler on No 4 *Edward Thomas* was condemned in 1963 and is seen here after removal from the frames, standing on an ex-Ffestiniog wagon and the frames of the first No 5, now used as a wagon. A new boiler was quickly acquired.

In 1958 *Edward Thomas* had been fitted with a Giesl ejector, a blastpipe arrangement designed to improve efficiency and donated by its inventor, Dr Giesl. It did not make much difference on *Edward Thomas* and was probably a publicity stunt to attract the attention of BR; an ex-SR 'Battle of Britain' Class 'light Pacific' was subsequently fitted with the device and was used on the 1963 AGM special. The metalwork of No 4's ejector wore thin and it was replaced with an ordinary chimney and blastpipe in March 1969. The running plates fitted in the mid-1950s are also clear from this view.

The 1964 boiler on *Edward Thomas* was condemned in 2001. For the final few weeks of its 'ticket' the engine was painted in BR plain black livery, which it might have carried had the Corris continued in operation. It worked a few photographic charters and is seen here at Nant Gwernol with the Corris coach and van in March 2001, 50 years since it first arrived at Tywyn.

Locomotive Developments

No 4's new boiler arrived at Wharf on 19 February 2004 on a trailer delivered by the builders, Bartlett Engineering. Without cladding, etc, it looks very small.

The easiest way to transport the new boiler to Pendre was to place it on the chassis, which had been overhauled while the boiler was being constructed. No 8 *Merseysider* has brought the chassis to Wharf; in the background work is ongoing on the restoration of the 1865 building as part of the station's redevelopment.

Fitting new tyres to *Sir Haydn*'s driving wheels. The tyre is heated over a specially made gas burner, the fire bricks retaining the heat. When the tyre is heated the wheel centre, hanging on the crane on the left, will be lowered into the tyre, which is then allowed to cool and tighten on to the wheel centre.

Once reassembled, *Edward Thomas* has a trial run to Brynglas, coupled to a down train hauled by *Tom Rolt* for the return journey. David Jones, the locomotive fitter, is driving, and works manager Martin Turner fires.

The 1970s: The Extension to Nant Gwernol

The mineral line east of Abergynolwyn was not part of the statutory Talyllyn Railway, though it was always worked as part of the TR. The TRPS always had the ambition to extend the passenger service along the mineral line to the foot of the first incline in the Gwernol ravine. A lot of legal work went into acquiring the land, then into planning the work needed to enable passenger trains to be operated over the route. Curves would need easing, gradients levelling and clearances improving; finally a Light Railway Order had to be obtained before work could start. The first blast was detonated by Tom Rolt on 3 October 1970. The project was managed by Bob Gunn, a mining engineer; here he and Robin Daniel are setting a charge. *J. H. L. Adams*

The 1970s: The Extension to Nant Gwernol

The conversion of the mineral line to a passenger line required that a 'contractor's railway' be available along the site. The 1865 track was in poor condition, mainly through the sleepers having rotted, and a new temporary track was laid, in part using the old rail. The new track is seen here joining the original track at Forestry Crossing

The temporary track is laid in the cutting east of Abergynolwyn, enabling works train to reach the various sites where curve and gradient easing was required.

The black shed served as a bothy and store at various sites along the extension, and here is being transported from Abergynolwyn on one of the ex-Bowater Railway bogie flat wagons, propelled by No 8 *Midlander*.

The final alignment of the running track would be moved south away from the top of the retaining wall at the east end of Abergynolwyn to allow for the extended platform. The hollow area on which the track would lie was filled with spoil from the various excavation sites along the extension and a temporary siding was laid into the area for the tipping.

Further tipping was required at the west end of Abergynolwyn station where the loop and west platform would be sited, and this rather insecure-looking siding was laid so that tipper wagons could be pushed along and the ground built up below.

The 1970s: The Extension to Nant Gwernol

One of the biggest jobs on the extension was easing the curve into Nant Gwernol station, at a site known as 'Big Bend'. The section from Winding House to Big Bend is on a ledge high above the Gwernol, which required widening and a wall building on the ravine side. To aid the heavy digging a second-hand Ruston 10RB excavator was acquired, seen in the distance with *Midlander* passing round the outside.

At the north end of Big Bend, looking towards Winding House, the temporary track has been slewed round the 10RB. *Midlander* approaches the detour, guided by Bob Lee. In the background is the former 'tea van', which was used as a mobile mess hut on the extension.

During the winter of 1975/76 the loop at Abergynolwyn was moved from in front of the station to the west end on the widened formation, and the platform was widened. The base for the blockpost has been built and a temporary siding laid to widen the station forecourt. The running line will be slewed to the right where the 10RB excavator is standing, and the platform extended to the east past the blockpost.

This is Abergynolwyn blockpost, showing the height of the slate-built base necessary because of the steeply sloping site. The room underneath is used for telephone equipment and storage.

The tipping siding at the east end of Abergynolwyn station: a toilet block would be built on the built-up site.

The 1970s: The Extension to Nant Gwernol

This view shows Abergynolwyn from the west during the winter of 1975/76. The platform has been widened and the track is being relaid. The east-end loop points will be where the ballast widens on the right. The gang are having a lunch break outside the station building, and the spoil siding is still in on the left.

During the laying of the permanent track just east of Abergynolwyn, a rail is being straightened using the crow.

At Nant Gwernol the platform edge is visible in the centre and a very temporary track has been laid along what will be the platform. The uprights for the fence at the rear of the platform are in place, and the 10RB is at Big Bend.

With the platform filled, work is going ahead to erect the station building, a wooden structure based on the building at Pendre. The original TR stations of 1866 at Pendre and Abergynolwyn were wooden; the latter succumbed to wind and weather in the late 1930s, but Pendre survived and was subject to a major rebuilt in the 1980s. A generator, a compressor and the mess van stand at the platform.

The station building nears completion and the permanent track is being laid alongside the platform. Sleepers are being laid out for the loop and the north end of the platform is being finished.

Looking down on the station site from the bottom of the Alltwyllt incline, fencing remains to be fixed and a fragment of the temporary track remains where the platform has yet to be completed.

Back at ground level and looking towards Abergynolwyn, track-laying is in progress. No 8 *Midlander* stands on the original alignment round Big Bend, whereas the running line will be to the left. The lever frame lies on the left and will shortly be installed to the right of the track.

While a rail is moved along on two bars on the platform tracks, Chief Engineer John Bate looks thoughtful, no doubt thinking of all that has to be done before the grand opening in a few weeks. The compressor stands at the head of steel, and the station building still needs slates on the roof.

With the loop laid and the platform being surfaced, a trial train is run to Nant Gwernol with *Dolgoch* and five bogie coaches. The station nameboards are up and seats provided – opening is only a few days away.

The 1970s: The Extension to Nant Gwernol

The blockpost at Abergynolwyn nears completion. The final slates are needed on the roof, the entrance steps are awaited, and the opening in the platform for the point rodding is in place; it will have a timber decking.

Before services were extended to Nant Gwernol in 1976, trains terminating at Abergynolwyn would run through the loop and unload in front of the station before propelling back to run round, then propelling back to load in front of the station. *Sir Haydn* has arrived at Abergynolwyn; the point rodding is now in place and the timber deck over its exit from the blockpost is visible.

A golden spike is essential for a proper railway opening, and Managing Director Bill Faulkner displays the spike at Wharf before the journey to Abergynolwyn for the opening ceremony on 22 May 1976.

The official opening train, hauled by *Dolgoch*, driven by Dai Jones and fired by Phil Guest, carried the invited guests. The engine was suitably decorated and is arriving at Abergynolwyn at the newly built west platform.

The 1970s: The Extension to Nant Gwernol

The opening ceremony was performed by Wynford Vaughan-Thomas, the well-known broadcaster. A platform was erected south of the line opposite the blockpost, and here Wynford (left) talks to Bill Faulkner and James Boyd, TR Chairman, before the ceremony.

With *Dolgoch* in the background, James Boyd introduces Wynford and invites him to open the extension. Treasurer Pat Garland looks on as the speech is recorded.

The blockpost provides a vantage point from which to observe the opening and the members on the bank opposite as the speeches are made and the line opened.

After the speeches, Wynford drove in the golden spike to declare the extension complete. The spike did not stay in place long, and is now in the Narrow Gauge Railway Museum.

Dolgoch heads the opening train along the Extension towards Forestry Crossing, watched by some photographers. Dai looks ahead to check that the crossing is clear; flashing lights would be installed here later.

Dolgoch leaves Nant Gwernol on its second trip of the day, allowing members to sample the new railway. The 10RB excavator had been left on the former alignment round Big Bend and provided a different view of the station. The contractor's track on the original alignment is still in situ today.

The 1970s: The Extension to Nant Gwernol

After the opening train had returned from Nant Gwernol, Mrs Elis-Thomas unveiled a plaque commemorating the opening, which is now mounted on the base of the blockpost. Dafydd Elis-Thomas, second left, was the MP for Meirionnydd. Wynford Vaughan-Thomas, with Mr and Mrs Boyd, looks on.

The extension runs through attractive scenery and woodland. Here *Dolgoch* runs past Ty Dwr, the site of the first engine shed and a watering point.

Nant Gwernol station is in the Gwernol ravine, high above the river. *Dolgoch* waits to return to Tywyn with the rake of vintage carriages; it has been painted in the 1946 livery that it carried after overhaul by the Atlas Foundry in Shrewsbury.

Nant Gwernol has no road access and to provide attractions for passengers a series of woodland walks was developed using footpaths and the former incline and horse-worked line to Bryneglwys Quarry. To increase the number of walks a bridge was built across the Gwernol south of the station; the land on the east side was in private ownership and the bridge and path depended on wayleave agreements. When the land came on the market the TR assisted the Woodland Trust to acquire the woodland and ensure public access to a very attractive wooded area.

4. To the Present Day: Commemorations and Celebrations

The Revd Wilbert Awdry, creator of 'Thomas the Tank Engine', was an early member of the TR, and created a narrow-gauge railway in his books, the Skarloey Railway, based on the Talyllyn. He drew on some of his TR experiences for the stories, including leaving the refreshment lady behind. In 1982 he agreed that the TR could run an engine as its alter ego of the Skarloey Railway, and here he poses with *Sir Haydn*, masquerading as *Sir Handel*.

Later Revd Awdry travelled in the Corris carriage, unusually marshalled at the Tywyn end of the train, and is watched by *Sir Handel*.

Sir Handel was not always popular with the children as he is grumpy and bad-tempered in the stories, so he was exchanged for *Peter Sam* (*Edward Thomas* in disguise), who was handed over at Wharf by Revd Awdry, standing alongside. *Peter Sam* was an altogether more likeable character and continued in the role until needing a new boiler, when *Douglas* took over as *Duncan*. While the purists dislike faces on engines, they are popular with the children.

Nature sometimes affects the railway. A flash flood at Brynglas on 10 June 1993 fortunately occurred shortly after the last down train had passed. This was the scene that met staff the following day, when the service had to be suspended for clearing up to enable one track to be used.

A farm gate is removed from the front of Brynglas blockpost, and the debris has been cleared from the track. The mud that entered the blockpost through the rodding tunnels was about 2 feet deep inside.

The Present Day: Commemorations and Celebrations

In recognition of the Talyllyn Railway's pioneering role in railway preservation, British Rail named electric locomotive No 86258 as *Talyllyn – The First Preserved Railway* at a ceremony at Euston station. It also carried the TR crest, which is visible above the nameplate.

After privatisation Virgin Trains renamed No 86258 to commemorate 50 years of railway preservation at a ceremony at Birmingham International station. Peter Bowes of Virgin presented the TR with a replica of the new nameplate, seen here with Revd Nigel Adams (left) and Roger Whitehouse (second from right), the then TRPS Chairman.

The two *Talyllyns* meet at Birmingham International. The Birmingham Town Crier joins Roger Whitehouse and Donald Heath after unveiling the plate on No 86258. Donald is a long-time TRPS member and driver, and was working for Virgin Trains at the time of the naming.

No 1 *Talyllyn* spent a period in the National Railway Museum at York after its visit to Birmingham. By coincidence it was positioned next to LYR radial tank No 1008; another of the class had been used on a TRPS AGM special in 1957.

Pictures of *Dolgoch* at Dolgoch are commonplace, but *Talyllyn* at Talyllyn is unusual. In late 2000 No 1 and carriage No 3 were the centrepiece of the Warley Model Railway Exhibition at the NEC in Birmingham, to commemorate 50 years of railway preservation. On a dull day the engine and carriage pass Talyllyn Lake.

21st-century Wharf

Here the traffic office and entrance hall are being rebuilt in the style of the original building. The museum and café remain in the background.

For a number of years the facilities at Wharf had been inadequate for the current business of the TR. Various flat-roofed extensions had been built over the years, the café was in a temporary building and the museum building was becoming life-expired. The Managing Director occupied another, and very damp, Portakabin-type structure. Moreover, the site is restricted by the two roads and the main-line railway. After a lot of effort a design was produced that met the requirements of a 21st-century tourist railway, albeit with a number of compromises. Funding was acquired from the Heritage Lottery Fund, Gwynedd Council and various other bodies, though not without a measure of frustration. The TRPS membership also gave generously.

The project was in two phases. Phase 1 was to replace the museum and café with a two-storey building containing museum, café and some offices. Phase 2 was to replace the flat-roofed buildings at the east end and rear with a rebuilt entrance hall, booking office and traffic office. The original building would be refurbished and continue as the shop. In the event Phase 2 was done first, starting in 2002.

One of the first tasks before work could start on the new two-storey building was to move the café to the south of the line near the gunpowder store. Continuing to run the trains with the work going on would be a challenge. Here the café Portakabin starts it journey to the south side, which involved two lifts. The museum would then be emptied and the contents put into store.

21st-century Wharf

Jubilee 1897, a Hunslet 0-4-0 saddle tank that came to the museum from the Penrhyn Quarry Railway, is prepared to be taken into storage prior to the demolition of the museum. The afternoon train awaits departure in the background.

With the museum demolished work started on the foundations for the new structure. The new entrance hall building can be seen beyond the original building and the café in its new temporary position. Railway operations were limited to the east end of the site and were complicated by the lack of a run-round loop, necessitating trains returning to Pendre to run round. The chimneys on the original building had been removed when the chimney breast was taken out, but, as the chimneyless building looked wrong, artificial chimneys had been put on, shorter than the originals. As part of the rebuilding they were restored to their former height.

Delivery to the railway is not easy, and most bulk items, including coal, come into Wharf. However, with most of the site now given over to the contractor, including the coal dock, there was a problem with receiving coal and with coaling locomotives. The coal deliveries were made early in the morning to Abergynolwyn and tipped at the top of the drive before being loaded into wagons using the recently purchased Bobcat. The drive was then pressure-washed before public services began.

The coal was loaded into the two MOD bogie wagons, with their sides raised to hold it. Each delivery was about 20 tons.

After loading the coal, the Bobcat itself was loaded back on to the ex-Bowater bogie wagon, known as a 'boflat', to be returned to Tywyn. No 9 *Alf* worked the trains, and care had to be taken on the down journey because of the weight.

21st-century Wharf

The steel frame of the new building at Wharf is largely erected. The upper floor is cantilevered out over the platform a little and supported on columns. The very limited length available for train operation is obvious.

With the building largely complete, and the framework for the station awning being erected, trains were allowed a little further down the platform. The chain stand on the right is one of the supports holding the chains used to control access across the running line to the café. The coal wagon stands on the centre siding.

No 6, running as Skarloey engine *Duncan*, stands in the completed station. The Matisa tamper and the flail-mower stand in the centre siding.

Tom Rolt shunts a works train at Wharf with the rebuilt station behind. The bogie van came from the MoD and is now the regular brake on engineering trains.

21st-century Wharf

Sir Haydn, in red Corris livery, leaves the rebuilt Wharf station. The two trains that ran throughout the timetable carried 'The Quarryman' headboard for a number of years.

The passenger approach to Wharf station. The new entrance hall is built to replicate the east end of the original building. The rear wall of that building has been restored following its partial removal when the flat-roofed rear extensions were built in the 1960s.

The entrance to the booking hall. The replica plate from No 86258 is mounted on the wall, succinctly describing what the TR is all about. To the right is the first plate of the electric locomotive. A large diagram explains to passengers where they can go and what they can do.

The north side of the museum's first floor is seen from the bridge over the main line – from this angle it appears to be single-storey. In a publicity shot a coach unloads 'a party' visiting the railway; inside they will find the museum, café and shop and be able to spend an interesting time until they join the train

21st-century Wharf

The TR was honoured to have the new Wharf complex opened by HRH the Prince of Wales, accompanied by HRH the Duchess of Cornwall. Having unveiled the memorial plaque, he is being thanked by TR Chairman Keith Theobald. Their Highnesses travelled to Wharf by train from Brynglas.

In an early editorial in the *Talyllyn News* the theme was 'No Names, No Hyphens, No Packdrill'. Highlighting individuals is fraught with difficulty, as others can feel left out. Many TRPS members have been involved for many years and have given yeoman service. John Smallwood is seen here (second left) commemorating 50 years of volunteering on the TR. John is not unique, and his involvement has included various roles involving train operation as guard, controller and blockman (signalman), traffic roster clerk, marketing implementation and carriage maintenance, as well as being a council member and director for many years, a career that he shares with others.

Maintaining the lineside and hedges in good order is a major task. In the early days two elderly men trimmed the hedges and cut the grass by hand. The Bomford hedge-cutter helped later and the grass was strimmed. The problem was finally solved when John Bate designed a self-propelled flail-mower using the chassis of one of the diesels bought for spares. Interestingly, the flail head is manufactured by McConnel, a family having connections with the McConnels who founded the TR back in the 1860s. The flail has proved very successful in keeping the hedges and lineside neat and tidy.

21st-century Wharf

A continuing supply of younger members is vital if the TR is to continue. 'Tracksiders' is a group where very young members can work safely on the railway accompanied by their parents. It is designed as a family event and there are usually two Tracksider weeks each year. In addition to doing work in a safe and supervised way, there are social activities for all the group. Many of the parents have already been active on the railway, but it does draw in new families and the volunteer base not only benefits from a pool of young members but also gets some older ones as well. Here a group work on the headshunt at Nant Gwernol. *R. Morland*

One of the many jobs undertaken by Tracksiders to help keep the railway looking smart, Zoe Morland is painting a milepost. In the background other Tracksiders clear the lineside. *G. Morland*

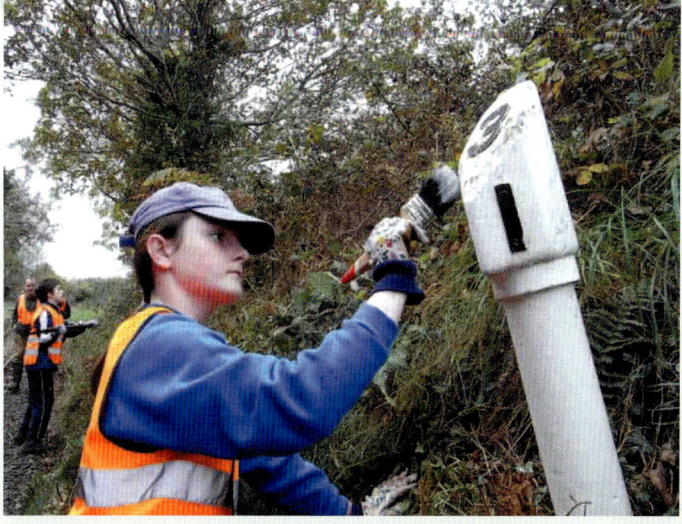

The TR Today

Though there has been much change at Wharf, Pendre and Abergynolwyn, not to mention the rebuilding of the mineral line to Nant Gwernol, most of the line remains much as it was built. *Dolgoch* poses amidst the daffodils at Rhydyronen on a photographic charter train with a rake of museum wagons. Goods trains rarely if ever ran on the TR, goods traffic being worked as part of mixed trains. The wagons used to be coupled behind the brake-van, but it is no longer permitted to have unbraked vehicles at the downhill end of trains, hence the van at the rear. *Dolgoch* is painted in a lined red livery thought by some to have been carried around 1900.

Dolgoch heads away from Cynfal Halt with the morning train on Easter Sunday 2009. Apart from hauling bogie coaches the scene has changed little over the years, although Tywyn has expanded in the background.

Dolgoch crosses Dolgoch Viaduct on the same day. Tree growth over the years has made it more difficult to photograph the viaduct, but pictures of trains in sun are possible in spring before the leaves grow.

A changeless scene: *Talyllyn* and the 1866 coaches run through Dolgoch woods. The locomotive is in lined black, a livery it never carried, but which looks very smart. A scene like this captures the spirit of the TR.

Photographic charters, which seek to recreate scenes of the past, are run most years. In this case *Edward Thomas* has had the running plates removed and has been 'dirtied' to recreate a Corris Railway freight train, though some of the wagons are of TR origin.

Each year on 14 May the TR runs a special to commemorate the founding of the TR and the first train of the preservation era. Guests are invited, and here the organiser, Chris White, is photographed with Major and Mrs Corbett. Major Corbett was High Sheriff of Gwynedd at the time and lives in the area.

The Founders Day special always stops at Rhydyronen where there are short speeches recalling the first trains to run there on 14 May 1951. Organiser Chris White makes the introductions while TRPS President Richard Hope looks on.

The TR Today

Special trains are often run for visiting parties. Here members of the Vintage Rover Sports Register pose with *Sir Haydn* at Nant Gwernol; the locomotive carries the Rover crest headboard.

Tom Rolt's many interests included vintage cars and canals. In June 2010 the Inland Waterways Association held a rally in Chester to commemorate the centenary of Tom's birth and the TR took along *Tom Rolt* to be part of the event. The engine was in light steam and its whistle echoed over the canal basin.

The TR celebrated the centenary with an exhibition in the museum and by running a named train throughout the season. *Talyllyn*, with 'The Rolt Centenarian' headboard, takes water at the old column at Dolgoch. The fireman tries to avoid getting too wet.

The last train of the Haydn Jones era ran on 6 October 1950, comprising *Dolgoch*, the 1st Class coach and the van. At Abergynolwyn the train was remarshalled with the van at the east end so that Mr Stretton-Ward could film from the rear. On the 60th anniversary of the event in 2010, the train was similarly remarshalled. Guard John Smallwood runs the van down onto the train, while *Talyllyn* runs round (*Dolgoch* was undergoing a major overhaul).

Locomotives have always taken water in the up direction at Dolgoch, but in 2010 a tank was installed to allow down trains to water. This was partially to save costs, as water at Dolgoch is unmetered, and also because the water there is thought to be of a better quality for the boilers. *Talyllyn* takes water as driver John Burton watches the level in the tank.

The TR Today

Maintenance is unending. Abergynolwyn station is exposed to the weather, and here the awning is being repainted by Dave Jones and Keith Hayes in the autumn of 2010 as part of the effort to ensure that the railway looks smart for the 60th anniversary events in 2011.

Dolgoch's 1958 boiler was condemned in 2009, but major fund-raising by *Steam Railway* magazine and the TRPS will ensure that a new boiler and major overhaul will be completed in time for the locomotive to star in the Diamond Jubilee celebrations. The new boiler has been built by the Severn Valley Railway at Bridgnorth. As part of the events commemorating the Diamond Jubilee of the founding of the TRPS in October 1950 a party of TRPS members had lunch on the SVR, and during the layover at Bridgnorth were able to see the partially completed boiler.

INDEX

General
Annual General Meetings 26, 36, 54
Bobcat 114
Bomford 'Hedgemaker' 68, 120
Centenary celebrations 73
Crich Mineral Railway 46
Engineering Committee 87
Fairbourne Railway 47
Flail-mower 68, 116, 120
Founders Day 124
Gibbons Bros 55, 60
Giesl ejector 90
Glyn Valley Tramway 47
Irish Turf Board 88
Jee's Quarry, Nuneaton 45, 73
Matisa tamper 116
Naming of BR locomotives to commemorate TR 109
Penrhyn Quarry Railway 30, 34, 113
'Tracksiders' 121
Weed-killing train 40
Welshpool 26, 54
Winchburgh shale quarry 75
Workman's Train Society 34

Locations
Abergynolwyn 12, 16, 21, 23, 28, 33, 36, 39, 53, 66, 73, 79, 81-3, 93, 94, 96-7, 101, 102, 114, 125, 127
'Big Bend' 95, 98, 99, 104
Brynglas 75, 91, 108
Cynfal Halt 122; bank 43-4
Dolgoch 19, 27, 56, 69, 124, 125, 126; Viaduct 25, 69, 76-78, 123
Forestry Crossing 10, 93, 104
Hendy Halt 74; bank 32
Nant Gwernol 89, 90, 92, 121
Pendre 15, 23, 27, 36, 39, 43, 62, 64, 65, 68, 74, 89, 98; carriage sheds 50-2, 63; loco shed 33, 40, 52, 84-5; Works 22, 42, 48, 52, 65, 85-6
Quarry Siding 5, 17, 18, 19, 37, 38, 45, 60, 83-4, 87
Rhydyronen 13, 21, 38, 122, 124
Ty Mawr bridge 17
Tywyn Wharf 9, 13, 14, 15, 20, 22, 24, 30, 35, 37, 39, 41, 42, 56, 61, 62, 70-2, 74, 75, 86, 91, 102, 112ff
Village Winding House 10, 11, 79-80, 95

Locomotives (TR)
Cambrai 61, 71
Jubilee 1897 113
No 1 *Talyllyn* 24, 55-6, 69, 73, 74, 110-11, 123, 125
No 2 *Dolgoch* 6, 7, 13, 14, 15, 16, 17, 19, 20, 21, 55, 67, 69, 74, 84, 100, 102, 103-6, 122, 123, 128
No 3 *Sir Haydn* 9, 20, 33, 35, 36, 42, 43, 44, 53, 83, 85-7, 91, 101,117,125; as *Sir Handel* 107
No 4 *Edward Thomas* 9, 10, 20, 21, 22, 23, 24, 28, 39, 42, 44, 53, 61, 62, 83, 89, 90-1, 124; as *Peter Sam* 108
No 5 (1) 22
No 5 *Midlander* 73, 78, 79, 80, 82, 95, 99
No 6 *Douglas* 29-32, 39, 42, 43, 45, 55, 66, 67, 83; as *Duncan* 116
No 7 (internal-combustion) 37-9
No 7 *Tom Rolt* 8, 88-9, 91, 116, 125
No 9 *Alf* 114
No 8 *Merseysider* 91

People
Abelson, Douglas 29
Adams, John 86
Adams, Revd Nigel 109
Awdry, Revd Wilbert 107-8
Bate, John 8, 22, 34, 41, 46, 57, 59, 66, 74, 88, 100, 120
Betjeman, John 73
Boyd, James 38, 40, 103, 105
Burton, John 126
Charles, HRH Prince of Wales 119
Corbett, Major & Mrs 124
Cuneo, Terence 68
Curwen, David 14, 22
Daniel, Charlie 84
Daniel, Robin 92
Davis J. J. 27
Elis-Thomas, Dafydd 105
Faulkner, Bill 10, 21, 23, 28, 47, 57, 62, 102, 103
Gardiner, Don 49
Garland, Pat 14, 27, 103
Gibbons, Eric 55
Glazebrook, Phil 65
Green, Snr and Jnr ('the Greens') 48, 49, 63
Guest, Phil 102
Gunn, Bob 92
Halliday, John 5, 60, 65
Harrison, Chips 34
Haydn Jones, Sir H. and Lady 7, 14
Holmes, Alan 8
Hope, Richard 50, 57, 81, 124
Howitt, Ian 77
Jones, Dai 43, 53, 69, 102, 104
Jones, David 127
Jones, Gareth 23, 24
Jones, Herbert 53, 84
Jones, Hugh 53
Lloyd, Jim 38
Meaden, Alan 64
Naylor, Geoff 21, 38, 40
Northesk, Earl of 29, 53, 61
Prosser, Owen 7, 11
Robertson, Robby 27
Rolt, L. T. C. (Tom) 7, 8, 9, 13, 14, 16, 21, 22, 56
Roobottom, Colin 71, 77, 78
Room, David 74
Slater, John 8, 26, 34, 51
Smallwood, John 120, 126
Snell, John 28
Theobald, Keith 119
Thomas, Edward 14
Trinder, Bill 7, 9, 13, 14
Turner, Martin 91
Vaughan-Thomas, Wynford 103-5
Walker, Major 37
Walton, Keith 5
White, Chris 124
Whitehouse, Pat 14, 16, 23
Whitehouse, Roger 109
Wilkins, John 47

Rolling stock
Allen chassis 30, 35
Bowater Railway 93, 114
Brown Marshall carriages 13, 42
Carriages: No 2 16; No 9 20, 39, 42, 43, 44, 78; No 10 34-5, 44, 78; No 17 49; No 19 78
Glyn Valley (Nos 14 and 15) 47-8, 61
Penrhyn 34, 36, 39, 42, 66, 75
'Tea van' 66

On 21 April 2011 No 2 *Dolgoch* appeared at Wharf on a running-in trip with the new boiler, prior to the boiler inspection the following day. With only three weeks before it is due to star in the 60th Anniversary events the team will be making every effort to have it complete. Here Nick Fieldhouse is working the reversing lever under the keen eye of David Jones who has done much of the work along with Dave Black, just visible behind the boiler.